# IN MANY FORMS

*a collection of poetry, prose, and lyrics*

POETREE

PTF

# IN MANY FORMS

Copyright © 2022 by PTF

All rights reserved. No part of this publication may be reproduced, distributed, or transmitted in any form or by any means, including photocopying, recording, or other electronic or mechanical methods, without the prior written permission of the publisher, except in the case of brief quotations embodied in critical reviews and certain other noncommercial uses permitted by copyright law. For permission requests, write to the publisher, addressed "Attention: Permissions Coordinator," at *contact@poetreethefeminist.com*

ISBN: 979-8-98603600-7 (Hardcover)
ISBN: 979-8-98603601-4 (Ebook)

Front cover image by Katrina Nskvsky
Printed in the United States of America.
First printing edition 2022.
*www.poetreethefeminist.com*

to Saeed,
for the dreams we deserve,

and to every person who finally found their voice after
being silenced for too long...

# Contents

*Dedication* v
*Preface* ix

I
The Introduction 1

II
Toxicity 59

III
A Dozen Roses 159

IV
The Butterfly Effect 191

V
Death of Ego 223

VI
A Flame 281

VII
BREATHE 331

VIII
Eyes wide Open 373

About The Author . . . . . . . . . . . . . . . . . . . . . . . . . . . . . . . . . . 428

# Preface

    I started writing poetry around 11 years old when I discovered that I could release the deepest parts of myself, with ease, by writing it out. At this age I felt so many emotions and in consequence created parallel faces to endure these emotions but over the years I quickly learned how to live *with* them. *In Many Forms*, explore the puzzle of these different parts and what colors them. It reveals parts of myself that I embrace and also parts that I deny.

    I know, unfortunately, society has systematized us to believe that the human experience requires only one way of being but the irony about it is even our human bodies are made up of many layers. We are like our earthly ecosystems. We have and need all parts, all roles, in order to make a whole. We were never meant to be one dimensional.

    It took courage I once never had to culminate six years of my writings into this book. I call it the moon in me because sometimes writing, or sharing it, can feel like hiding under a blanket with a flashlight, scared to be truly seen, calculated on when to come out or go back under.

*In Many Forms* is a reflection of how I wear many hats and the discovery that wearing many hats is a superpower. It's a dive into my truth, my fears, ambitions and dreams. It's a stamp of learning and unlearning and of rediscovery. Overall it's the backbone of my inspirations and stepping stones in my creations to date. It's an example of the power in how I push through hard times when they come.

While compiling these chapters it was kept in mind to encourage my readers to be their happiest self no matter what, that means putting self first even through the hardest times; a reminder to feel all their feelings because they're valid. I wanted this to be a reminder to stand strong, be proud in bearing strength and to welcome the lessons learned because that is ultimately all that matters.

The goal? To motivate to create.

> "you were created
> and thus
> you must
> create"
>
> *In Many Forms*, Chapter 4: The Butterfly Effect, p.203

Finding ways to intersect multiple qualities, or many hats, of my creativity is just a reflection of the intersectionality of my identity and I embrace this.

Color and movement are also pieces to my puzzle and can be motivated by what I see just as much as the emotions I feel. It takes awareness and intuition to connect the two and this is expressed through the chapter cover visuals.

I try to bring whatever I see--whether color, dance, words, or even my hair, to life from the very loud pictures I experience in my mind. I say I feel like my energy comes from some divine feminine tree, deeply rooted in the earth, that remains green throughout every season because even in the deepest and darkest of times I still pull through with blind faith. The process is the real journey and I want to leave footprints with these pieces from *In Many Forms*.

This is a personal reflection of my current healing journey, direct and robust. It is the first installment of a three-part series featuring poetry on love and actualization through time and the divine feminine.

I wrote this series of short poetry, prose, and lyrics over six years, a wild ride through my young adulthood, to reach out to the hearts of all who have felt lost *and* found, low and high, and everything in between. It's for the ones who can't explain how they feel, the realizer, the go getter, the reflector and the learner. This is pure heart.

As the first of three, this collection dissects the many levels of *self-love* and how it can **grow from any soil you choose to nurture**, from self-acceptance, intimacy, epiphanies, or relationships to the realities of depression, anxiety, abuse, sexuality, or identity.

*In Many Forms* is separated by eight chapters each representing a different layer in my path to growth.

### The Introduction

This is the beginning. This is where I take my first steps in being and feeling. Everything feels as big as the first step a toddler makes or the gush feelings from the first day of school. It's filled with unknowing.

### Toxicity

Here are seen and unseen problems within self and relationships. I process it with turmoil inside and outside. This chapter feels like a sinking ship as I realize the plummet can come as quickly as the rise.

### A Dozen Roses

Appreciation. A way to give credit when it's due, I move through how I would "give roses" to loved ones and inspirations, eventually seeing things for what they are.

### The Butterfly Effect

The ultimate cause and effect. It's reflective of balance while describing the imperfections of life, love and the people I come in contact with but still seeing the beauty within them regardless. It's not perfect but it's beautiful.

### Death of Ego

Release. This is about lessons learned and overcoming obstacles within. Our minds can create what may not actually be there. Nevertheless, I needed it in order to overcome.

### A Flame

All about courage. I discover that fear is inevitable and experience peaks and valleys of overcoming my fears by leaning on my courage and later, added faith.

### BREATHE

Faith. Walking in faith takes more strength than expected. This is when I start to become more trusting of myself, others and God.

### Eyes Wide Open

Awareness. The only way to navigate is with three open

eyes. I learned that awareness came with intentional silence. That is when I heard my voice the loudest.

The purpose? For the process of *metamorphosis* and the willingness to uproot for the better. Growth can happen if we allow it space to move.

I hope you can recognize yourself here.

# I

# The Introduction

the beginning.
taking first steps
like a young child.
It's the first day
of school feels:
first day of
work,

the
inter
view

the
audi
tion

I'd rather be a poet
With alphabetical books that explain love
                        And all its counterparts.
That show love in the mind
                Body
                      And society.

The root of all things great

Is love.

I'd rather be the poet who colors your mind with words and emotion,
    Bring you tears
        and deep devotion,
Have you think
About loves corrosions,
Have you wanting to pick up a book

                and understand
The meaning of        words…

so much more than
                its letters

If I could taste the honey
that drips from your flower,
Everyday,
I would be full
Of sweetness.

A tree
With hard bark,
Sap under her chest,
Roots that rest,
Under the moist green grass
That feeds her everyday.
Carvings of "i love you's"
That only fingers know
The joy of.
Cherry buds that decorate
Her pretty,
And dew,
That tops her irresistibly.

The crickets from last-night
Left me lost in green sound,
Palpating my green heart.

Love,
          like water,
      as satisfying as it is
Choke me when excessive
And drown me when possessive.

If there was a way to give myself love
in physical form
It would be where bees
make love,
Where sunflowers grow,
Where grasses dew,
It would be me looking back at me.

After every heartbreak
there is healing,
scars
That work just fine,
Just like old skin.

The best thing about emotion is the passion.

How we can be engulfed in every feeling, fill with tears when we're angry or hurt, or bend in aching pain from laughing so hard.

I love being passionate. Whether "too sensitive" or "overreacting" my feelings are mine.

Take every opportunity to understand the root of your passion even when your passion leads you wrong.

If my nectar is sour to you
    Too bad.
        I can produce gardens of flowers.

Mountains move slowly darling.
    And when the ground cracks
    So does my voice
    Because even the highest eagle can't
    Equate to the level my screams reach.

Friends,
Like stings from a bee

move nectar       to nectar

And die after one bad touch
leave you running but interested
absolutely necessary to life.

Family,
Like scars that heal with time,
Is none too perfect either.
I hope they appreciate your pollination.

Whatever I told you
I meant every word of it,
That I am a gem, but you can't see,
That I forgave, after everything you did.
That I'm open even though
I don't want to be.
But you keep breathing,
Like I was just a hiccup.
yet
You don't hear me
But my heart,
You're still keeping.

This life of mine will force me to walk down a road harder than most. I will be cut but I will walk.

Why can't you understand that
This spontaneous combustion
That I call my heart
Is yours?
Every time I start
To feel every pump
Blood flows,
Endlessly,
And I fall
hopelessly into you.

That is what life is about:
Living everyday
As if I love to live.

you smell of grape popsicles
Laffy taffy, the pink kind
Nerds
The pink too,
and the purple I could never find

                              it's the smell of flowers
                              Of Capri
                              Sunflowers

Strong and sharp red like fire
Fighter like bumble bees
Flower
Like leaves on trees.

## Nork

Brick brick brick
Brick by brick
This city is cobblestoned with
Greatness
And pain
But painless
You be
When it's time to stand up
bulk and raise buds
Flowering
Brick by brick
We hold up
Sometimes we hold down
But that brick sound
is the finest
brick by brick
Brick brick brick
This city is timeless

~ nork kid ~

**It's so feminine**
I fear it
so
I escape to masculine energy
Hide in masculine energy
Survive in masculine energy

The feminine feels
Like nakedness
And
a fight with a beast
hands tied

I've had emotional pain
That hurt more than my tattoos.

Pain is relative.
It exists if I believe in it.

A black sheep
That had no home
Black, and filled with grit and envy,
Had big brown eyes
And was strong in size.
Black, had known his weight was heavy.
He had black written all over.
black.
Marvelously evil
they say
and above.
they say
Less than,
Not enough,
And ugly to the core.

*And what else?*

**Woe is me**

No one will believe in my vision
Until i bring it to fruition
And then
they"ll want a piece of my fillings

This moment
I feel my eyes
Moist
With tears that wet my cheek,
Hug the top of my lip
While I kiss you

a poet when i speak
    when i write
    when i dance
    when i cry too

Save myself for you
Not my flower but My mind.
That part is open,
Not my legs,
Vulnerable...
For you.
I will protect my Yoni.
As soft and welcoming
as she is,
Worth all my treasuring,
Put her away.
She's worth all my worshiping.

Fill me up
To the brim
With words of encouragement
Cause I'm tired of
Being reminded of my flaws.

Be gentle,
As you are with me,
Hug my heart,
Pick my brain,
Wipe my tears.

She said:
"Sweet chewing gum
Let me pop your bubble"
As she ripped off my wrapper
Ignoring my labels,
My ingredients,
Hopping right to my flavor.
Displeased because
She didn't take the time to read.
Since she can't swallow,
And my bubble is weak from discomfort,
She spits me out.

No amount of time
Can be enough
To mend
What are pieces
Under my feet.

Calloused with strength,
I walk,
No matter the cuts
Because growth comes with
Struggle
And struggle

teach
Lessons.

If what I see in the mirror
Is what you see in me
Maybe I would smile a bit more

There are different modes
To my madness:
The boil behind my eyes
That burn you with a glance,
The silent cry that hurts my
Throat
And stomach.
Cries so loud that they're nearly quiet.
Then the rage in my throat,
The worst of my madness,
Where I say things that
I'll regret later.
The soul tearer,
My madness,
I'll regret later.

my sickness
And my medi-
cine.
Yet I'm yearning for more
To open eyes and ears

The more I feel disconnected,
The more I learn to deal with disconnection
Rather than fight for reconnection.
You'll lose me,
A part of me, more or less.
What's worse?
I'll lose myself.

Growing inside of me?
bones and organs
who will dance for your arrival
Genes and blood,
That could be everlasting love?

*the future*

My mind,
Bent,
To the ends of time,
Squished,
With memories of you.
Hurt,
me more than you do.

The greatest thing I've ever done
Was fall in love.
It was solid proof
of my openness.
Willingness.
And even through betrayal
It was great.

Father,
I wish you could see
The woman
I am today.
Your flaws would have meant
nothing to me.
                        You could've seen.

Ma
I am not a spitting image
Of you.
and that's okay
as much as it is a blessing

Losing you
Is more
Pain than I
Can explain,
my friend.


*highschool memories*

I've settled
    too many times
For those, who couldn't
Speak my love language;
for those who didn't understand.
So every time
It was the same ending.

If I never accepted
My flaws
I would have never concluded
That I am
A "once in a lifetime"
Whose lips speak truth,
Body produce life,
Mind create truth,
Whose eyes create vision
for the visionary

What a curse
And a blessing.
I should never lose control
So loosely,
So blindly,

*uncontrolled*

I affirm this:
I am a black woman
I am a beautiful black woman
I am creativity
I am life
I am love

Depression as real as real is
can break and be broken,
shake your physical
but
broken pieces
can be
     picked up

You were my best love,
And worse pain.

If you do not feed my mind
only satisfy my body,

Beware.

If I give you the time,
Sorry.
My intentions may be ill.

Still.
What you cannot do
Another will.

Journey to the L
Hug with the O
Live with the V
Elevate with the E

Generous
With my heart
Even through
My anger.

I said:
    Fall in love.
I'm selfish.
    I admit it.
I want you to fall in love.
    Let go of all your fears,
    Fall in my hands,    and melt like putty
Between my fingers.
    Warm like heat in winter.
satisfying,
    Like a breeze through thick air.
Absorb my kisses,
    Care
        For my heart,
Because you know I would too.
For you.
Fall in love.

I vow to dedicate my life to truth
— have I not kept this vow?
Will I lose my faith?
Will I let me down?

The magnificence
of intellectual
 beauty.
 Why do you think
 The fall
 was so hard?

Love is my choice
that I sometimes deny

turn a cheek to

A choice that I sometimes make
Irrationally,
That I lock away
Hopelessly,
That I embrace
Happily.

My roots,
You cannot be.
My eyes,
You cannot see.
If I were to blow in your wind
Would you still hear me?
Would you read me then?
If I wasn't what you expected,
And gave
You stimulation,
Bended imagination,
That you confuse for simulation,
That green, not as green
As I,
    simply your reflection.
    Would you still hear me?

I was that flower.
Uprooted.
Trampled and forgotten.

Thorns cracked
Pedals scratched...

Can't stand
But did.

Dragged myself to the nearest soil,
Pushed myself in,
Covered with brown to my brow,
Watered,
Loved,

And then began to grow

handcuff the brain,
    order it to pipe down.
slap your heart around

    Push it away
        to never be found.

lie to your reflection,
    say everything is okay.

and you'll find
all the answers
Written in the tears
on your face.

# II

# Toxicity

I think revelations
Are lies
In disguise.
Realizing what you
Already know
Is no
Surprise.
Repeating it
Is just hypnotizing.
And leaving it
Is just depriving.

                          I said it more than once,
I love you.
                Though I shouldn't have to repeat,
And you shouldn't have to ask

Sometimes
I see you
In the reflection of my tears,
crystallized
and Salted with fear.
Moist lips,
Wet, below your hips
and tears
I can wipe away.
but
You I can't stay away.

I prefer cries in the shower

The water so loud
I can't hear my thoughts

And that how I like it

And my tears wash away
Down the drain
As if it never happened

I also realized,
though,
That love
Is about letting go.
Even when it's the hardest.
Because the last straw
Is the one that weighs
The heaviest,
And do the most damage.
Throw.
That straw.
The farthest.

If they tell you you're wrong
	For your feelings,
Your mind,
	And your heart,
They are blind
	To your being,
Your essence.
		blind to your heart.

**When i look in the mirror**
Is what i see
The truth?
Or is it the culmination
of what I make up?
Is it how I feel?
Think or assume?

i've been thrown away more than I've thrown away

Until my body allows Me to become a parent
I will not be yours
I'm too occupied
Being my own
Anyways

Actually,
Why do I credit you for what my mind has done? Didn't I work hard for my sanity? Didn't I work hard for my truth? Didn't I work hard to understand that love starts with *me* and not you.

Would I recognize myself
if i grew
with
just
one
pedal?

I must like fire
Because I play with it
And burn.
Then turn around,
And do it all over again.

Rumbling.
I thought it was easy to
Overcome
Stumbling,
For you.
But I'd rather have bruises
Than find out I could lose
You.

Blood boils just like water do.
If they cared
They'd be there.

Baby,
I remember fighting for you
Holding buildings for you,
Flying for you.

Baby,
Calling baby,
And crying for you.

Maybe,
If I didn't hide from the truth
You wouldn't of had
my time
To lose.

Love can be a bit obsessive, right?
It takes over your mind,
To your very last thought.
Control your actions and
Reactions.
It tells you lies,
When you need it most,
And let you cry
At the smallest refraction.
It slaps you around and judge you,
Yet it's still so beautiful.
Running to love,
When Love is a drug,
It's hard when love
chooses you.

Sometimes when rocks are thrown
                I'd reach down, pick them up
                              And put them in my pockets.

I guess I'll just hide
Behind
Glitz and glamor & the sparkles enamoured
       with little white lies
That keep me smitten.

I guess it's real hard to follow a path that's already been written

I guess I'm less of
Whatever I already think I'm less of.
Riding
On a shimmery road to nowhere
Until I stop
Hiding

**You never have interest**
But expect
To have
The privilege
Of being involved?

Sometimes I want no one.
How content I am with me,
How much I love myself.
What can someone else give me
That I don't already give myself?
How can you see my mind more than me
Or love me more than me?
Be true to me more or not,
Lie or be unsure?
No one can give me what I want more
than I
can.
That is my my pain and my mercy
Because others can easily desert me.
And I'd rather have me
Because I deserve me.

I was told that I pushed too hard
Even if it was for their benefit.
I pushed too hard.

I loved too hard.

I tried too much.

But I guess
A flower that
Blooms
Widely
Would be envied
By the ones who couldn't.

Even if you came into my life today
I would not deny you.
For if it were me
you would be true
So I trust you

to be truly you.

an elephant's back
        Is as black as coal
    Yet perceived as grey
           When they're dry.
They wonder too
        And love like you
They kiss their kin
        And wash their skin
And though their skin
        Is different from others
They never let that bother.

I cried
And cried
For a long time
Weeks maybe
And my old self
Was washed away

Everyone's too busy
      Being cool
           Looking
                Cool
To be

cool

Name
Me
As
You
Wish.
I
Care
not

What is it that I see
That others cannot understand?
How different am I
From others
That walk straight lines of control,
Nod to command,
And let go of their souls?

if the screws are loose
The foundation is shakey

I'd rather you be real and cruel
Than fake and nice

denounce the expectation of access
with
    no
        real
            relationship

Thinking is for royalty
Who let greatness shine
on their jewels
Blinding the ignorant.

Royalty,
Being those who are awake.
Jewels,
Being the truth they shake.
Ignorance,
Being those who only take.


Thinking is for those who are awake
Who let greatness shine
on the truth they shake
Blinding those who only take.

*High or Dry*

I'd rather not
Play childish games
And go insane
With crazy thoughts,
or
Assumptions
Of the unknown.
I'd rather you tell me freely
Whether you see me
Or would rather leave me,

You cannot have me
On your time
And your time
Only
You cannot love me
sometimes
On your time
Only

if this show ain't for you
exit left
And then find another stage to
satisfy your chest
before you clutch your pearls with me
because this show here
is freedom
being
free

If you're so bored
Because
This is balance

healthy

And equal

Perhaps you should go
And find your danger

if you take
Bar for bar

It's a replication

A copy we say

Don't expect gifts from
the same place
You so freely take from

No respect
To approach
And ask or be curious
or to give the place a chance of choice?
You just take
And then
Cry for the place to still give
grace for the sake
anyways?

I can feel how much you don't love yourself
I can see it in how you show up for me

Glad the glow.
Unfulfilled, the girl.
Silenced,
The Box.
Keyed and locked up
With long scratches on bolts
 And cold feet
Cause it's old.
The box
The silenced box.
Gladly, the glow
He sped up, she said no
He kept up, she said no
He's fed up, she said no
She said no.
She said no.

*hurt to live with*

you welcomed the anger
That filled you up
When my anger filled up
When I stood up for myself.
Rage
For finally not fawning to you.
This scar is yours.

giving grace to the land
Of my mind
In which
Volcanic eruptions
causing disruption
Only brings in the destruction
Of what needs to end
Because then
I could rebuild my land
Again

How upset I am
When I review all the good times
Because now I'm brushed with the bad.

Unsatisfied you were.
That even now you'll revel in
with these words
That you recognize
To be yours.

Maybe you're blocked
And you just can't tell
cause
Your eyes closed
don't even try
because your mind
Is the one
Who chose
For your heart
don't know who i am
cause
You don't know who you are
&
un happy?
Happy?
Unhappy people are not happy about happy people

probably blocked

I am not yours.
Don't you dare take away
What rightfully belongs to me.
This body is mine
And so is my mind.
As well as these curves,
And every other word invisibly written
On my kitten.
Pouring sparkles of love
That I know overwhelm you.

So you can say what you say,
And thus tremble at your ankles.

You can take what you take
Because you think I can't shake you.

But I don't stay
Faithful to unfaithful.

Last summer
    I hung off a cliff
            And I watched you
                      Watch me
Hold on for dear life.

You saw that I was strong

And decided not to give me your hand.
        and when I made it up on my own,
I thought,
How delirious
I am
To stand
next to you.

If I gave you the blueprints
To the house
That holds the love for me
And you never used it,
you can't blame me
For demolition

when sex was so hard
Because
R
Engraved inside of me       pain
I knew not
my own
 pleasure

Crabs crabby crabby
They snap snap
And be aggy
They snatch snatch
and do it gladly
Yank and pull as you wiggle to climb
Yank again
When you start to incline
snap snap at each other
snatch snatch
then run for cover.
never tipping over the bucket
it's surely shabby

but a
Crab gon be crabby.

**crabs in a bucket**

**in no rush**
But want to hurry
As i watch the time fly
By me
Quietly and
Loudly
Ignoring my every
Signal

Chasing with no catch

And then
when i wasn't giving
the
Last
of my drops
suddenly
I was unworthy

But only to the eyes
Seeing from
the Outside

Honey molasses.
My heart
That bleeds sweet
Juices.
Pumps through sweet lines
That lead to you.

Through thick diamond
skin,
That's uncut,
I want stickiness
For your sweet sin.

Teach me what you must
And then be on your way.
I am perfectly content
With your expiration date.

distaste
on my tongue
for those who
Had the door
To pour
    Love and unconditional
But simply

Chose not too

Those cries hurt. The ones that pull at my gut and irregulate my breathing. The ones that make my vision blurry. The ones that hold on tight to my throat until I feel a sharp pain of regret. The ones that stop my heart and pull on my mouth.

The ones that stain my shirt
and hurt so badly
that they have
no sound.

There I give again...

Embracing the whisper...

Without me
An emptiness...

Remember missing
Each charming dust?
Calling fresh winter?
Engulfing fragrances?
That lingers,
Breaking,
Tender?

Don't forget,
Please,
That I get angry too.
I get low,
I get weak,
I wanna leavel,
and I wanna leap too.

poor choices

you call mistakes

Rainbow your emotion.
Collapse your memories.
Jealous your eyes.
Question your view.

Pros and cons of growing up with very little

Con
Having very little

Pro
Seeing love in everything else

*intangibly until 22*

Trust my existence.
Dance to my song.
Desire my toe-tipping,
And touch my dripping
cloud.
Deny these rumors.
Raging beyond vibrant sound,
Serenity,
Folds perfect softness,
Deep surprises,
When this existence is found.

Without
The softness of emotion
lives imperfection
Catching a special
Kind of lovesick,
That's cold sadness.

I still carried you home
Drunk, hurt.
With all the dried kisses
On your neck.
Laying wet in the grass
After you stood me up
After you pissed drunk
And I cleaned you up
And went home,
By myself.

True
These struggles
And sorrows
Shine light perfectly.
Buttery breaking
Burning forever
Summer sharing.

Let autumn rise!
Black sugar run lonely,
The color of my life.
Quiet girl
Whose heart uninvited
Wandering her fragment,
Surrounding fear,
Crave fiercely,
A lost you.

My confidence,
To fully cover
And conquer,
Turn heads

Let me tell you
I am as strong as the wind that whips your face
Make you wrap so comfortably around me,
My finger,
But in the most positive way.
In this, you can unwrap yourself whenever you want
And I'll understand.
But I'm still here when you want to wrapped again.

Because like water I am
Too
Satisfy and nurture you too
Kiss
Ing
Melting lips
See
I'm the sweetest sin
Sent free.
But I'm a criminal
Because
i'll make you fall in love
Then leave…
So magically…
I'll rob you of your ignorance
And pump you full of knowledge.
But once you know yourself well
You'll move on to another topic

But i don't stop.
I keep stealing and stealing
Hearts that need healing and mending.
Love that needs shaping and fitting.
Let me tell you
I'm a criminal.

Living now
Is like teeth pulling,
Hair pulling,
Toe jams on table corners,
And paper cuts.
Small but big pain
Inevitable but necessary

I am a lover
But never loved how I deserve.

I fight with every word
in me.
And kiss with every breath I have.
But I
To them
Am always incomplete.
not enough.
too much.
And so I sit with empty hands.

One day I woke up with a wet face, wet pillow, dry mouth. I lay stuck and struck with sudden pain that I didn't feel. I didn't feel it, but I did, and I, early in the morning, skipped breakfast...and lunch...and dinner. Back to bed I went with a wet face, wet pillow, dry mouth.
How dare I waste away another day.

*-Depression from a Broken Heart*

To whom I thought I should be,
And who I thought I lived
and should die for.
To whom I wish I tried more,
Who should've tried more.
But neither of us did,
And I cried more.

My **anxiety** likes to hug on my bones
    As if i invited it
        Welcomely
Like i like
Conversations while sitting     in fire
Free   free   free
falling
without parachute attire

it's panty hose tight
    Hugs on my off white insides
And on the waves of my nerves
    To the connections of my neurons
and
i get too gone
I'm not alone
anymore
I got hugs
all on my bones

And so if I'm not breathing
Believe me
It's the reason

told
That I wasn't enough.
Lucky for them,
I didn't remember their name.

The lines of
mental,
physical and
emotional abuse.
I'd rather break those lines.

I am... today and every other day, my own enemy.
Stuck under the moon
With the light blinding my innocence
And the night chilling my soul.

The breeze that blankets me
And the truth the stars show
tells me I am my own enemy,
I am,

Tear down myself.
Lack of presence when I need help.
Lack of faith and
The less I felt.
But
Now I am willing
To enemy slay

I need a doctor who will do their job, fix me physically.
Await my reactions.
I only want the best, the youngest, the fastest.
Why not?
I'm worth it? Aren't I?
It's a special job. Now and then questionable. But yes.
It's like this.
"You're fine"
"No, I'm not"
"You know this"
Now and then, I do. But Doctor gets frustrated. He repeats.
I take a seat.
A hard road of thick words spill from Doctor's mouth.
There I am. That's what's important.
I control me.
But Doctor's words control me too.
It hurts.
It hurts.
It hurts.
I've tried to get over it.
I'm serious, I have.
Keeping up with myself. Accepting myself.
I think, doctors are God,
God controls his words,
Words are God,
has God rejected me?
"You're fine"
Sometimes a person, lost like me, gets lost infinitely.
Doctor is here with strong hands on mine.
And then I leave.

You see
Because I was hated for what I'm loved for now
I have. I have. I have.
Mad. Extremely.
At nonacceptance
Doctor, please fix the problems
I'll feel much better.
"You're fine"

Sometimes a person, lost like me, gets lost infinitely.
yet, I control me
But Doctor's words control me too.
Doctor, who's glad to be of use
Focused, cautious, meticulous
Confident in Doctor's words but a bit rude
Sometimes, yes, ridiculous, and obtuse
Really, almost, almost always a ruse
I'll grow old ruing you
I'll grow old in spite of you
Doctor
I'm worth it, aren't I?

*what's on the outside*

**codependency**

**is**

The fight between the act of fishing
&
The comfort of giving fish


Fishing is self love
and only giving away fish is lack of self awareness


    self sufficiency

If I could take this pain into my heart
And spread it through my veins
I would be sick,
SICK,
And filled with dark matter.

If my energy is too much for you
Why are you here?
Why are you raining on my
Self made fire
Of life

Deep diving
Head first
Into the abyss
                This swim is deadly

I thought
If I pretended to be okay,
Then I would.
If I pretended to get over it,
I would.
But there's something
Deep,
Caved and carved,
Inside of me
trembling
To let go.

Screaming
With no sound
How could you not hear me?
If you cared to listen,
You would.

**so much has been stolen**

my innocence
My voice
My smile
My experience
How could you not
Hold on, for dear life,
To what you have left

I wanted to record more

Because

"I ain't never been nowhere"

and

"I ain't never seen anything"

**I look some eyes
right in the face**

At times I can see
And feel
how much
They do not love me

Even when they pretend
It's exquisitely
Exhausting
To pretend with them

As life seems like a stage
sometimes

I have nothing to say
Mums the word
Be I
It's the silicone verbs
That's stinky stinky
Pink eye
One eye
Now you can't see
Cause It's disguised
As real vibes
But I realized
Have nothing to say

two legs for walking
we only walk for ourselves

Some people chose to sit down
or lay down
when they fall

but it's a choice

scared all the time

If it's not the anxiety or intrusive thoughts
It's worry.

 in a constant battle
Looking for what I called "love"
But was really

safety

the entire time.

To be and feel
safe
Has not been a motif
In my life.
To survive and fight, over come
Create
Encourage
Build and conquer
I am

But safe?
I can count very few times

I can keep this all

feeling
Feelings
Inside

And it can burst at the seams

down from the beginning,
That I was willing to hold you up.
A lifter who isn't lifted
Falls too.
So I gracefully parted ways
with you.

a ball of hate in my pits
so big
I can give birth to it

Knowing that you can move along
As if nothing happened
As if he didn't die
As if..he was never alive
in the first place

Knowing that
It will be just the same
when i go too

always got an attitude or

know how to dampen the mood and

energy is the only proof

**Vice versa**

People love when you up
And hate when you down
People hate when you up
And love when you down

**10/30**
**What Control Looks Like**
it's real confusing
Because
Everyone everyone everyone
Looks alike
And
Everyone everyone everyone
Speak alike
They kinda think alike
They share words from left right
Tumble in real fake fist fights
They steal words
And walk with the herd
Turning that mind volume down
And that INdividual down
That indecisive, indirect, deflective
Mind
Attracting possessive reflections
Hypnotized by rounded lines
Those Blurred lies

But life is a reflection and collection
Of your choices too
Not just outside noises
Not just outside voices

You want some meaningfulness?
Don't treat yourself like shit

Say: "I'm allowed to change
I'm allowed to change my mind
At any given time
Regardless of fuss
Because I AM what happens when the sun and moon make love"

Blind to it..
.

Is this a spell?
Cause If you're not paying, you're the product baby
Is this a spell?
Because What you see as slaying,
I'm just saying
Are just the puppet masters playing
Hanging
Strings claiming how you feel,
how to think,
who you are
No wonder you can't see your scars

Sometimes
When I'm lost in thought
I get lost in pain
Caught by dreams
That trick me.
They're colorful nightmares
Of taking long dark stares in dirty mirrors.
Why can't you love me like how other mommas love their daughters?
Fathers with their daughters?
I know you were young
And
It's hard being a parent
But
it's okay being transparent
It's okay to be caring
But instead of carrying a 9 month bill
Should've thought about all the skills
That bill had the ability to possess
The stress you thought was a job
Was a blessing
Now you're not understanding the lesson
Momma when I asked you to hug me you forgot
Father never been daddy
And all my feelings for you stopped
I started to sulk and ask why I'm not good enough
But I am

I've always been

Hate lives so deeply within us

That is balance.

and
If we allow it
It sure can

Be stronger than love

# III

## A Dozen Roses

*When I Pray*

Omnipresence.
I see it in the earth.
The way the trees move,
The way the sun hugs me,
How the blood in my body rushes,
How the silence feel.
Sometimes tears flow when I'm in pain.
Sometimes I spill questions from my lips.
Other times, I am thankful.

Beauty is not about
Who is better.
No one is and
We are all
Don't you love your family
Not judge them?
care and uplift them?
have your spirit with them?
Beauty is nothing without the mind,
Adverse or not,
If I am not favorable
I know by whom I am.
Along with being my own fan.
You need not compare to these unrealistic limits.
They're fables of the impossible.
And lost files of the probable.
The Probability of your beauty,
Compared to fairytale limits,
Is like trying to swim through trees,
Impossible.

what i love about creation
Is that
It exists
In your mind first
As tiny fuzzy letters, pictures and colors
The clearer it gets
The wonder that comes
Is through your hands
when
these tiny letters, pictures and colors
finally come to
Run together

I exist
To give,
To breathe
Life onto.
To fly,
To soar
Deep within.

**Ancestors teach me**
Courage lead me

I never knew
What true love was
Until I laid my eyes on you.
Your brown face,
And light weight,
Were Mine for take.
Your big smile,
And first steps,
Left tears on my face.
Your first bath,
Your first words,
Now I look up to you.
I never felt love like this,
Until I laid my eyes on you.

*-my brother's keeper*

I love you more than could be explained.

It takes a lot of courage and effort to maintain a relationship
let alone
for years at a time.
Thank you for your time, effort and love.
the point is less about fancy things, rules or even expectations
and more about enjoyment, respect and grace.

Partners are those who agree to hold hands through the walk of life
and I could not
imagine holding
anyone else's hand...

*hey*

I am not this pretty pretty girl
That's only for show and
Looks.
Jewels that shine
Brighter
Are worth more
The dirtier the dirt.

What's the word?
I hope you're having a good day
and those cracks that
Split
On each side
Of that
Very smooth face
Stay put.
And the looks you give
When you don't get your way
Goes away.
And the fate
That changed everything
Is best,
Even for you.

I just love to wrap my face on it
The way we glide
and indulge in our favorite tastes
of honey.
sometimes it's fast
But every time, each time, it's real deep
and it lasts.

I just love to wrap my face on it
And then do it again
Because what's life if you ain't living?
What's love if you ain't shifting?
True honey
That's you honey
More than money
I want you honey
And if the misrepresentation
is temptation
Let it be

Cause self love
Is a hell of a drug

Falling in love
Is easy.
Staying in love
requires work.
   *A motto*

**I would be a bold face lie**
If i said that all who i loved, friend or not
I don't love anymore
I would be wicked
more than the west witch
truly
I would be stricken
with cold cold ice box
For my heart
Cause every body
I've held
I've loved
& love still

Can't be a light switch with my insides

i admit, though
my body knows how to
Turn off
And on

One day,
I wanna touch a cloud.
Feel
To see
If it condensates
Between my fingers.
See if it's soft like they say
Or invisible as science has written
Is it cold?
Subzero cold?
Even in the summer?
How does it hold
All the water
to the maximum
Then
Just
Let
it
all
Go?

You see we're just like oceans
Bodies of waves and lumps
Bodies that can drown you
and your emotions

I was told,
by many birdies,
to fly high
as high as I can.

fly

they gave me the words
in their precious chirps
but if my wing is broken
where am I to go?
if my glide is low
 how can my color show?
when it's finally time
how can I fly?

You can be defeated,
But not destroyed.

Hey,
You remember the stars?
The open space?
All that green?
And dinner for two?
A night of TV
and
Walks beside streams,
Puffs of smoke,
And strokes of my hair
When I was in pain?

*sunshine*

Do it again?
Say it again?
Risk it all,
Again?
The piles and piles
Of loving,
That's stuff down down.
Love that's only recovered after miles
Of running.

*lessons*

You
Are
every pedal that wraps tightly
To my core.
every level
Of love that peels
And feels
Because you water me right.
My thorns mean nothing if
Your hand is calloused.
And my scars scorned
Are just directions that
 you read well.
My pedals are softer when they
Brush your hand
Multiply by the dozen
Even in the winter

Your hands, my soil
Your hands, my soil

A bird
That flies broken winged
Is not crazy,
But willing.

*herself*

    Pedals Dried
Is like hardening
For the softest flower.
Lasting longest
Like lovely scents
that Devour
On the hour.
So No need for water,
Quite quenched they are.
Colorful,
They are still
Lovable,
They are still.
    Lovable

the electrocuting
Protruding,
Soft pink lips
That make my insides
Like pink matter.
And on my nose,
Sweat back flips
With lips warm
moving glitter all over like sun rays.
Tastes on my tongue
Feel like a tiny dangerous speed chase
And navigates on every follicle of my body.
You're somebody,
Your kisses are something.
And I'm hooked in.

*sunshine*

I think I found my Aphrodite
Cupid,
Looked out for me.
I am hooked on your ecstasy.
Falling Virgo,
I think I'm a whirlwind
Rising Leo.
I am wild sin.
Shining Aries.
And the sun doesn't burn me.
It swallows me whole
and reflects me

*sunshine*

I saw a huge blue wave
That couldn't touch me
But I still drowned.
It said
    'I am here, in your face, to reveal'
Of what?
I was lost,
    'Truths that you choose to ignore,
    your zeal.'
The blue wave turned purple,
Then white.
And I realized that the blue wave might have been right.
I drowned because I allowed it
When I can easily swim.
And I ignored all my greatness
Because I thought I wasn't worth it.
yet here I am,
Trying again,
Near a big blue wave.
    "I am here to reveal"
and I am here to stay...

I have me
a gem
That God dropped
down on my lap.
So easily,
And lightly,
All I had to do
was accept

*sun-*
*shine*

**of all the dirt**
Plants grow here.
Love your soil

Support is like water for
the flower.
She is nurturing
With the roots being love.
Are you watered?

We should always perform acts that will bring about the greatest happiness or the least unhappiness for other human beings. The consequences of what we do, then, count for everything; we have to take into account both short-term and long-term consequences...treat other people's happiness as *equal* to our own.

## Human Project

I.m.p.e.r.f.e.c.t
the human body
with our 5 senses or
6, if your 3rd eye is open,
We live life...

Never do we honor
the imperfections that can sometimes
launder dark, so called love
longer
in our spirits,
& Under our skin,
destroying our stronger
parts

In the name of self love
wake up.
Cut the strings that hold
you to your old
dance.

the puppeteering
shouldn't have a chance
to jerk you through the elastic trance
of control.

In the name of self love,

we must honor our senses,
your common sense
& every ability to sense.

Because your imperfections
can never measure.

pleasure
Is getting up
Every morning, healthy &
Feeling better

It's the feeling of water
nourishing your insides,
& the sun shining upon
your face.

The little things,
The human body,
Us human beings,
We live life.

# IV

## The Butterfly Effect

I

I wish I can flutter on your mind again.
Feel your skins
Like we're fine again,
And again,
And again,
Cause all we did was float in circles.
Same flower, different garden.
Same pollen, different center.
A different center.
Now you're winter.

2

In the sky
I am the colorful wings
That fly pass the pain.
Yet my eyes sting with regret
If I go too fast.
Thorax full of swallowed kisses,
from a kiss too fast.

My antennas shifted,
I'd rather be on the grass.

3

And now I sit,
Full of content,
But before
I could pull my hair out.
I accept,
I embrace,
How life tends to shout
Big "no's" and
That I'll never have all control.
So I'll just fly with the wind,
and I'll still grow.

*4*

Being broken winged
Is painful
But it is not
The end.
still
a butterfly
is made to flap regardless
in the winds.

5

Sometimes
 you can't tell what's right
From wrong,
Blinded by
Pretty colors.
You go the wrong way,
Make the wrong turn,
And yet would do it again
Without a stutter.

I refuse.
no one
Flaps my wings but
Me.
And I will fly,
Where I please.

Love is but war
And all its thoughts but schemes.
Smiles that have cracks
That break
at the seams.
Seams that fail
To hold together.
The two lips that make you moan,
And the headaches,
That turn heartaches,
That turn stomachaches,
That rip the flowers grown
for the Garden full of casualties
It's a war you never asked for.

even as a dancer
I've learned
there is power
In stillness

As a poet
There is power
in silence

Looking back at my younger self
I feel light and darkness
As we both burden
The heaviness of
Similar weights
and these weights are tied tightly to ankles
and wrists
working with water
to engulf
us whole
with our truth
leaving with the bubbles back to surface

thankfully today

it's seen these weights are loosely tied
and when i try
i can swim again

I'm a flower with many petals on it
Living through many stages
In life and death
And then all over again

**Afraid to die**
and afraid to age
Ultimately
It's the unknowing
That eats me alive

I admit

Feels like I've gone nowhere
But am
still
so far from where
I was

You were created
And thus
You must
Create

Wake up feeling brown
Being brown
Alive for many lifetimes
I can mourn those
Afraid of the sun
Afraid of real passion &
heat the soul
Mourn those
Who choose to ignore life
Ignore Mother
Whose ground
Brown ground
Made you and I

to not connect but
Just stagger amongst
ourselves
with metal in our hands
Flashes so blinding
That we're on stage
Playing the role
To play
Unreal the crowd is
for they are robots
powered up for entertainment

the definition of who i am changes all the time
Because i change all the time

morals and ethics in tact or improved

a definition?
sits on a spectrum

When i cut my mane
I gained new clarity
Resistance to resistance
And welcoming
To change

**puzzles have many pieces**

Intuitive work is the direct bridge to creativity. It's literally where it all (should) come from, even when it's not intentional.

but intentional intuitive work is unstoppable.

I'm willing to walk away
Or walk to anything
I want or deserve
Simply because
**I'm built different**

giving the silly me
As my (inner) younger child self
Was
& Is
But only for the people
Who make me feel the safest
To be

....i realized that I lean a little too much onto my masculine energy, which I love deeply, but live too comfortable in, and whenever I am too comfortable I can be stagnant for a little longer than needed.

There is growth in (the process of) discomfort but also, just because I am used to something it doesn't mean that the latter is worse or will forever be uncomfortable...

I stayed snuggled in my masculine energy because, it was me of course, but also because I needed to, for safety & protection, reassurance, discipline and assertion.

My feminine energy was hidden for survival...and survival came first. But now, I am living, feeling and being. I know right now I can learn the deepest layers of myself through my feminine energy.

*fem and masc ENERGY*

In rediscovering my fem I can find the happy balance of what I need from both fem and masc. Not what I have to be or think I should be. But who I am.

It took years but my path is mine. Balance is the goal, my balance.

*Goy*

Lately, I keep saying I'm in a cocoon...because I am. I'm in a whirlpool of emotions, ups and downs, sadness and happiness, figuring and finding new ways to grieve, let go and grow. And it's always the same cycle just with new faces. The ecosystem of self evolution.

Elevation over Stagnation.
The mind is too powerful to waste.
Nothing can destroy what is already at peace.
Once you realize that you have control over yourself and your life more than you think,
   life finally becomes a journey.

## The Holy Trinity

What's in your Brain. What's in your Mind.
What's in your Heart.

Many people think of the brain and the mind as being one of the same thing. Both are used interchangeably, but I think they are *separate* and distinct. Our brains are visible and tangible. Our minds are invisible and transcends into thought, feeling, attitude, belief and imagination.

How can the mind and the brain be the same? What about the heart? Your soul? Do you need one for the other's existence? Do our souls just house the mind? Can you have a mind without the brain or have a brain without a mind?

Our minds
are *developmental*, shaped by our surroundings, our relationships with others, our emotions, and our personalities. It could change, grow or stagnate over time.

Created from many variables, it may just be an expression of the soul:

your love,
your hate,
your confusion.

The invisible soul that transcends into other intangible parts of
self: our feelings, our character.

What is certain, though, is that the mind evolves with time
and the soul
leaves the body
when the brain ceases to function.

The Holy Trinity

—balance is the goal—
Kindness is not transactional
It's a gift without regret.
Balance is the goal
Because It's always a coincidence when it's a bad thing
But a miracle if it's a good thing
But everything is meant.
We have control over our kindness so
Please don't mistake that with your niceness

Things last as long as their supposed to last
Not as long as you
Want
Or hope
them to

The conflict that raises inside
Of me
Knowing that I don't
Fit the conventional way of being an artist
Of being
What you see as a womxn
What you see being beautiful
What you see as being


The conflict that raises inside
Knowing that
 the conventional way of being
a womxn
a man,
or any other human being
Does not truly exist
Actually
And is not my truth
anyways

Covered in flighted beauty.
The butterfly is
Because he's of this earth
Not from.

But the him in her
Is way too masculine
And the gentleman in him
makes him question
His divine feminine.
Even with beauty brushing pass his eyes

And he chooses

to fly away

Take a vacation from normalcy

Winter is for hibernation...don't be afraid to sleep, recharge, regenerate.

When spring has sprung you will feel just like the flowers who bloom
    like the butterflies bursting out their cocoons.

POETREE

# V

## Death of Ego

Hello,

I'm your past.
I just wanted to stop by
And tell you to keep going.
I know I pull your hair
And I know you still care.
Just accept,
Then let go.

There is no wasted time in lessons learned.

The strength I found
In all of this,
These shackles
That hold me down,
saved me.

I've realized it's true. That I am selfish. I indeed put my own energy first. I make decisions that's best for *me*. Sometimes that comes with jealousy:
    because fear pacifies self love
    creating the perfect environment for envy:
    Malleable while weak.

In all, I remind myself that I shouldn't wait on anyone to make me happy
    the right people wouldn't have me waiting around.

> Hey,
>   I love you, first of all. I'm sorry if I held you back at any time for any reason. I am still learning. I'm grown, but I'm just a kid, you know? At the core, I just need. So sometimes I'm great and other times I don't know what the hell I'm doing. I think that's what life is about... just doing, just needing, just wanting. It's not about yesterday or tomorrow. It's about right now. I missed a lot in my young life but not focusing on the now and I don't want that for you.
>   Live for right now love.
>   Nothing is permanent but your spirit love. Love endlessly but not foolishly. Give widely but not until your cup is empty. Put yourself first because I know what it's like to not.
>   You deserve everything you want and everything you don't even know you want and deserve.
>     I love you
>     You deserve life
>     You deserve abundance
>     You deserve peace
>   Through it all, I am with you

We're all searching for something to give meaning to our lives.
Look inside.

I thought
If I tamed the fire, just a bit,
It would not burn me.
But it hurt more.
I thought
If I play nice
The snake won't bite
Yet my tongue burns with venom,
I thought
I was lucky.
But I was trapped.
And I happened
To undo
The latch
In which I thought was a seatbelt
But really,
was a noose.

There's an art to losing yourself
As much as
Finding yourself

So many piercing eyes
i melt sometimes
Inside
when i can't handle
i mask sometimes
feeling safer when i hide

Mistakes taken
As a woman
Who grows
From the concrete of pain.
She lives on the handprints
many left while the concrete was still wet.
She takes these memories
As a lesson more than anything.
You can't have success
Without the love for failure.
Though hard,
The concrete is,
She remembers to tell you that
She keeps the handprints as her own.
The helping hands for what she can't do.

Sometimes I treated other people how they treated me.
It didn't make me feel better but more empty.
More hurt. No matter what.

So I focused on maintaining my heart.

you can't expect people to believe in you more

You have to believe in yourself first

I also learned that vulnerability comes from the root of trust. So when I don't trust myself or my decisions it tends to reflect in my relationships. I used to see it as:
" I don't trust them" and
"I don't trust anyone"
but really it was
"I don't trust myself in the decision to trust them"

No matter what I can't control other people, just myself. So even when I trust, it's taking a chance, and that's for good or bad.

I now trust everyone, but I trust everyone to be exactly who they are.
I trust myself to make the right decisions for myself when the time comes, whether from good or bad situations.

It always comes back to self

You go low
I go to hell

That's how i was
real immature shit

But I'm not that anymore
After looking my shadow in the eye
not even it
can take me down

Wake Up.
awake.
Up in the wake
Of an eye.
I see you but
You don't.
Won't you stay?

trauma
   The leftover
   of the past
offer
fear
   stress.
      and a door

**I admit**
That as a kid
And young adult
I was impulsive
explosive
Aggressive
But it served me well
And i carry the water
Of lessons
That grow me
Today

Thank you.
You were the hardest thank you
To swallow.

*The Past*

You cute

But what's your personality?
Your purpose?
Your thoughts on thoughts?
For thoughts sake

**A journey through my shadow**
The downs and flawed aspects can either be changed or not.
This path is discovering the role I play in my own suffering,
    in someone else's suffering,
       in the downfall of things
A conversation ensues between these many pieces unashamedly.
Freedom is produced when accountability exists within vulnerability

I'm sorry I'm such a poet.
I can't hide my poetry.
I can't hide my words.
I can't hide my heart.
How loud it is

*Anger*
Let me go,
I am so tired.

*Love*
Hold on,
I miss you.

*Passion*
Don't stop,
You fuel me.

I feel

Sometimes i have to hide behind the weekend
It's the safest place to not be

When I meditate.

I imagine a white force beam of light all over my person. Everything beyond this beam is absolutely mute. Inside, I can hear myself breathing, I feel my breath slide off my lips. I hear my heartbeat, feel the squishiness under my eye lids. I can feel my blood rushing through my body like waterfalls. I can feel all the vertebrae along my spine sit tall. I feel it all. And then I feel nothing.

*Restful mind.*

To be at peace,
I open up
To myself.

to be seen through the eyes
Of beauty only
Is a fleeting thing
50 years from now
the eyes that now see
what they've seen
will be
something else,
will the feelings fleet too?

Death creeped in

took
And snatched from my hand
I thought was everlasting
But
never was

*grieving so deeply*

Grieving old me
As she
Dead and gone

I can emulate
her,
though,
Cuz I've walked and talked in her body

But

It's just getting on stage
Reciting lines
that I've memorized
time
and time again

I can grow a garden out of nothing
my resourcefulness taught me
through my struggles
and survival.
But if I had a garden firstly
Oh
I wonder what it would be
to make something from that


*scarce*

If all you want to see
Is the pretty
And not the ugly,
For I am many parts,

Goodbye.

The path to success
Is a bumpy one.
Many, that may slow you down,
Hurt you,
Change you,
Improve you,
Make you think
Differently.
learning that there is more than one turn
on your path
If you just look up.

resentment is the garden of weeds

When we don't forgive we leave our garden unattended
Susceptible to ruining our soil.
If we don't get on our hands and knees
Take the time
To pluck the weeds from our garden
It can never
Go any further
Than the seed
Under soil

A plant thrives
When it's time
To be
In a bigger pot

Water with no space
breeds weeds
Of discomfort

I don't raise my voice to my queen
I leave that
    energy
    when needed
    for pure strangers who bring danger
threatening my existence
or protecting others when needed
but to my queen?
not even the last thing

    *I'll do*

Waking to please you?
Let me live,
Without you.

You see,
Worthiness
Is a funny joke
You see,
Because it's subjective.
Yours not theirs.
somewhere in the middle
Doesn't exist

I'm a poet.
Poets don't let things die.
We record it,
Forever.

I've dreamt once
Of healing powers
Beyond
Imagination.
I healed the young
I healed the poor
To every satisfaction.
then
A figment of you
came along,
With all of your baggage,
Asking for help.
The god in me
Told me
To put aside the hurt I felt

I drunk
My anger away one time,
With my pain right along with it,
Because I was so tired of feeling.
I wanted to drown
Even though I swam well.
 I wanted less
Even though I deserved more.
My hangover,
Hung me over.

    *pain is inevitable*

Honey let this go
They will be a part of your demise
Not
Your
Rise

I am on a journey
That will cause
Many losses

Is her mouth too much?
Is she too loud?
Too loud to connect?
Bite your ego
Or brush your self respect?
Living
Breathing
Fire
That boils pain
Is she too much?
Too much to tame?
Ego dead or renewed
It's all the same
Is she alive?
Fire so soft
She learns to flow
She learns to fly

I could act like the toughest person
Or smartest,
Most talented,
Or most loved.
But I can never fool
My reflection

My life flashes before my eyes
And tell me everything I think I always knew
That I'm in control

& all my words are true.
Blind to my woes
Who are stricken cold
In heat too deep to fathom.
Cause closed ears will never hear the truth
Or entertain mindgasms
Because
It burns the eyes
Chokes the throat & shakes the you
Out of you.
And damn
My eyes water
And damn
My life flashes
But the ego can hold like glue.

**Never hit first**

If you hit first, everything after will be determined by the other person.
If they hit first, everything after will be determined by you.
No matter how hard the situation, there's an opportunity to take control.
Will you dominate, eliminate, renovate or educate?
Whatever you think, you are right.

**defend**

**I wouldn't want to be known for my pretty**

It's flattering and I could, in its simplest level, do just that. But that's not what drives my soul. How I look will change every year passing but who I am, my purpose and soul given impact is what lasts forever.

My true legacy.

I've been holding a lot of weight, grieving, growing and building all at the same time. It's very uncomfortable but I know it's not impossible to get through. The process is harder but I'm doing my best. Gratitude gets me through.

The lessons of enjoying the journey are highly popularized in order to create motivation. It's easy to say the journey should be the real focus but hard to live it day to day. It's hard for me too.

The only being I am better than is my old self

I cannot compute
Every aspect of who i am
Every fiber
And tool used or unused
was prescribed
and described
As
"You cannot"
Yet
Here i am
I'm every "can't" shoved down my throat
& I make it seem like
I'm not even choking...

I make it seem like
I'm not even choking

Conundrum
Sometimes
I wished i could see
Me
Through the thin eyes
Of others.
The envy
And the lovers
Anything
But
Empty

i had to fill so much of me,
By any other means,
In many other cups
Always against my luck
Reeling in the constant loss of sight of my true identity.

Then other times
I saw the small light
I reached
And i reached
Until i was still reaching
And I'm
Still reaching.

And that was me

rather be lost in light
still illuminating even when the dark comes by

than be blind on the wrong side

and i may change my mind
But i know
My light remains the same

10 years ago I was angry
8 years ago I was clueless
5 years ago I was curious

Today, I am in the most important transition of my life. The road less traveled. The lonely road. The hard road. The painful road of looking my shadow self in the face and holding their hand. Smiling at discomfort because I know it won't last forever. Accepting growing pains because it is elevation over stagnation.

always growing, adding and subtracting from my old self...

**Depression is that friend**
You don't want around
And trust me
They will hold you down
Wrap you up in expectations
And then add weight by the pound
Look like you but don't feel like you
But don't live like you
But don't trip like you
Commit or fit like you do
But those looks
The twinkle
In their eye
They hide in the wrinkles of
Your mind.
You don't want them around
Trust me
They'll just hold you down

**If I'm going to be seen**
I want to be seen
With meaning
with value
And intangible power

Malignant
Ignorant
Attendant
Suspended
Tinted
Winded
Defended
Committed

And making
Decisions
with other Visions
within massive Tensions

Moving with no
Engine

Just
Wishing

I used to think I had to be

a sense of happiness for the growth
a sense of sadness for what's left behind

if they say they don't like me, believe them
if they say they like me, believe them
I've lived many lives already
each revealing a different layer,
different pedal
    different phase of my being

    they may have experienced depressed me
                    jealous
                    vengeful
                    angry
                    spiteful
                    immature me
    they may have experienced happy me
                    grateful
                    generous
                    spontaneous
                    vulnerable me

these are just some of my pieces.
and they have just one

                *the past*

# VI

## A Flame

To deny
Is to be afraid.
So I think I've learned
The second layer of patience:
Acceptance.

*sunshine*

Surprise me!
I know what I want.
Unexpected love,
New food on my tongue,
Strong spirits
Who teach me about life.
How life
Is love
And vise versa.

2

How soft you are when you
Whisper sweetly.
Sweet chewy candy,
Your lips
As pink as taffy,
You make me
Laugh with no worries.
*You taste like freedom,*
Ripening bananas,
And jellybeans for the soul.

excuse me as I'm busy discovering me

Oh, how I love that you
Allow me
To feel
Exactly how it comes,
And you hug me after,
And you paint me with love.

*sunshine*

chilling
On the same clouds
We debate over.
It's warm like the sun
we question during sunset
And inviting like the green
That keep us breathing.

*sunshine*

Time is medicinal
**my time is expensive**
It heals with patience,
Logic
And rationale.
Intangible
Blind and
Quiet,
It's the line that holds us
Tightly
To the universe

**It's real to feel**

Before, I functioned as an emotional codependent, so what I thought was vulnerability actually wasn't... but now, I know I can be vulnerable when I allow

1) when I have the emotional *capacity*
2) when I *trust* my own *intuition* about the person or space
3) when I'm *aware* of practicing emotional *regulation*...

In other words, when I'm putting myself first, safely and without harm to others, I am ready to be vulnerable.

I'd rather a steady incline up
because rockets
Fall back to earth much faster
than when they started

It's difficult for me
To make a name for myself
if I
carry you along with me.
Wanting more for myself
Makes me selfish,
And you,
You're filled with bloodshot envy
And pity
Because you think
This is all for show.
But
I show only beauty.

And I want only to spread it,
To every heart that's willing to have it.

Unfortunately,
And fortunately,
I am a product
Of my trauma.

*Blunt-forced*

when my cup doesn't overflow
I will not pour too much out
Or thirsty i will be
And the bottom of the cup
I'll see
And be
Dry dry dry

It's like hip hop poetry
Not street jazz or phoniness
Just real facts and flowing
Fits
Real tips with honesty
Honestly
It's rhythmic
Just like your heart
Two beats back to back
With the same kind of parts
Parallel
It's side by side
All around
It's the air, water and ear drums
It's like hip hop poetry
rhymed for rubbing
nickels, sides or bottom  bums
It's the sum
Of revolution
Photosynthesizing
your children
raising your 3rd eye to
Poison
Protecting your mind
from closing
It's like hip hop poetry
Made to listen but
Dance to too
It's like hip hop poetry
Rhythmic rhymes doing
What rhymes do

**Pick and choose your battles**

Legs are for walking
Cars are for getting to close distances
Planes are for crossing water and long distances.

Leg does what the car and plane can't do
Car does what leg and plane can't do
Plane does what leg and car can't do

Everyone plays a part

Many parts of a whole

**You watched me walked the steps**
Then demanded i come back down
Put you on my back
Walk back up
And put you beside me

i would love you here
But you must walk up
With your own legs
So that we may meet
And continue together

I thought
without a hand
Holding my back
I would not succeed.
Look at me now

so thankful

                                                              For the lessons

That beat me

                                                               Into shape

Like clay

                                                           Where would I be

If I was made so softly?

**The universe**
Is
So funny
And validating
Even when you have no confidence
it'll remind you

More than just a game—

And then i realized
That i am no background piece
No pawn
Or even knight
no rookie
Or down for bull-bishop
Not even the king
with no value

I am
the queen

I remember cold, snow, dark nights and shivers.
 I remember warm, sunny, shining soft colors.

left me falling.
    let me down.
        I accepted it.
            I moved on.

they

Cannot identify with he but can
Identify with she but don't

they feels like home
But it's heart pacing

it is
just a part of me
like the hair that grows from my scalp

They

Just like when you first dip in the pool
So transitioning
So extreme
So cold

Until it's not

And you're swimming underwater

There's a difference between

what you're good at
what you're passionate about
what you like
what you love.

It determines how much care, how much attention you give, determined longevity, and possible outcomes

Only the defeated wolf
would cry out
after the sheep
finally turned
Predator.

when i walk in a room
I walk head high
With confidence
And buckled faith
with bold assertion
And

You can Feel this beauty and love
But also understand
There will be no room for
for disrespect
Or finesse

No sort of act
I need to put on
To impress people
Who probably disrespect
Or finesse
At any chance they get

To say what i want
Not what others want
for my want

Even on days
That remind me
of my losses
I still have faith
That God will
fill me up
In other ways.

I knew and they knew it was always inside of me
The way it was responded to?
Is different from then to now

**Who not how.**

Whenever I run into a problem I don't think about how to solve it I think about who has done it before

I'm sorry that i have substance
That i have a heart
A mind
That i give a fuck
That i
Don't give a fuck
I am not an empty vessel walking
I am a spirit
guiding a vessel

    Not sorry

Admit when you're wrong. There is power in failing.

                                                  Release the bonds to trauma

Bounding you to the wrong side of yourself

I don't want to do anything that supports
A condition
In my being
In my creativity
I want to be unconditionally me
I deserve to be unconditionally me
No boundaries
But self boundaries
Whatever i say
How i say
When i say it
Autonomy
Over my mind and body

if you don't f with my art
You don't f with me

— love me —
I hope you forgive my delay
My laid off time
My day off days
As that's my way to keep sane
To stay relevant to me
To elevate my free
To hesitate when needed
And protect as I see.

**If you not rollin**
How I'm rolling
I can't f with that
If i smell deceit
In my street?
Scratching
Better yet stabbing
My back
A fact
I'll tell ya
I won't loosen up
This grip will thicken
on both my thumbs
If you not rollin
How I'm strolling
Tell me,
Where you going?
Back back
I guess
Back back
to the
other
side

my love story .....

   ...first taught me to Respect myself
   ... second taught me to Protect myself
   ....third taught me to Love myself
   ....next taught me to Trust myself

As our own bizarre fears can become a prison enslaving us like a moth to a flame.

How can she fly if they
Never teach her how?

**I don't have to be in shambles**
In order for you to support me
Just because i hold pain, struggle and ugly
Well
Does not mean
It's easy
I don't have to present
What is perceived as weakness
In order to receive
support, love or tenderness

The more I refuse to accept
My own greatness,
The harder it is to believe
Others when they see it.
And I get tearful,
and fearful,
Because my imagination
Creates outcomes
That will never actually be.
I draw up conclusions
That disagree with logic
and time.
Ignore my Divine
Femininity.

Forgive me.
When I wake up
From this blinding confusion
I will rule inevitably,
My mind,
With no intrusions.

**Don't Fall in line**

Don't think I'm crazy
Cause I'm not
I'm just about ugly truth
Those Loud ass truths
Like Morpheus said:
The red pill, if you wish

But that's you
If you'd rather have the blue

I bet they won't tell you about
This potion
This beauty is love and devotion
this movement is poetry in real motion
Explaining
That each c u r v e is just
Another direction
Up the mountain
To maintain
This spontaneous combustion
of color, garden & evolution
Of destruction, reconstruction
And introduction
To the dEYEmension
I bet
They can't explain the passion
Because it's only meant to be
Felt
Screamed
And ripped your chest
This potion
Poetry in motion
Is inside

**They don't know how to deal**
Because they don't know how they feel
But I love to evoke emotion
Cause turmoil and mental commotion
whisper in your ear long rings
And pull on your heart strings

Life is about your mindset
    What you believe, you see
        What you see, you believe
    And you if you could see & believe, you can do

Success gives you choices
    YOU are the chooser

It's time to be a vessel
to hold your purpose
at the pit of your belly
And the very tips of your fingers
To stand up for what you believe in
Have Heart, Logic
and Reason,
Breastfeed your achievements
breathing
the very air
that born you
don't lie in boredom
every time your fed up
live with your chest up.
and embrace your pleasures

Crazy talent always comes from the streets.
You can buy technique
but you can't buy soul....

My roots
You cannot be
My eyes
You cannot see
If I were to blow in your wind
Would you still hear me?
Would you read me then?
If I wasn't what you expected
And gave
You stimulation
Bended imagination
That you confuse for simulation
That green, not as green
As I
Your reflection
Would you still hear me?
Would you read me then?

My feelings
both
transparent
and
a brick
Wall.
Neither penetrable,
With hands or mind
And that is my flaw.

I have demons too.
I just choose not
to feed them.

*Me too*

I'm not sure
If I'm ready
For what is
planned for me.
patience come
And hold my hand

It's okay to be indecisive. I like to believe that our brains process feelings through our hearts at times. The confusion stems from a mixture of logical thought and compassion for others. This causes us to get stuck at a stand still when these two forces argue.

I embrace this mixture.

If I can explain
How much joy you give me
In words
Hundreds of years
Of library paper
Would never compare.
    If I could tell anyone
How soft
Your kisses
Make me feel,
That you fill
Me with lovely smiles,
    And hand squeezes,
And Hershey kisses,
They would smile too.

*sunshine*

I am troubled.
And I ignore this part of me
Because of my ego.
And I ignore this part of me
Because of my fear.
But what I learned is that
Fear only exists because *I let it*

Life is like crossing the street

Imposter syndrome is that space between leaving where you've been and going where you're meant.
It feels uncomfortable because you've never been there before
but
it's where you belong.
You don't know how to...until you do,
but you belong.

Connecting with you in spirit and heart
And mind
So that
Even when we leave this life
We can still find each other in the next

If you're looking for the wrong answer you will miss the right one

in the saddest but most truthful way
No one will care
Until you do

Will you use the stones you have to build stairs
or hold them all in your hand?

faith
& courage
Scream much Louder
Than any fear

Unfold your heart.
Pull it apart,
Spread it,
Tame it,
It needs,
So badly,
to b r e a t h e.

Each level of growth or success are equal parts not definitions. When a new level comes, it then takes you to the next level. Your goals can be achieved step by step, if you allow.

*the journey*

can you be the seed
and the tree at the same time?

i'll go
cause
God's my light
and my sight
this is all I know

Growth is just like a plant...
If the pot is too small
for the roots to grow
The plant will die.

Regardless if you water it

worked so hard to prove
You can believe in me
So that people could believe in me
But then
Nothing moved

Until
I believed in myself

Pain is meant to be felt
Your attitude determines your altitude

losing my right ear hearing for some time

it was like god said
You will listen or you will not hear at all
I never noticed that
I never took the time to truly listen to my voice
All the way down to the vibrations

I was hearing every note, crack and flaw
Humbled
At the force that said
"This is you"

Ironically building me up
with character and confidence
After breaking me down
with fear and truth

This is who i am
Because it's engraved in me
It's Not what I portray for view
But Too little understand
The heavy hand
Instead of Holding my hand
As i follow
My God written plan

Will I allow my past to destroy me?

Will I allow my past to consume me?

faith talk
      vs feelings talk
           vs failure talk

Words are either poison or fruit
Words kill or give life

rather be happy and
Without
Than unhappy
And with.

It's hard to fight pain,
and hurt,
With compassion;
Genuine passion
And understanding.

In what world
Does it not burn,
Under your skin,
To still be good
To those
Who are not
Good to you?

we constantly compare ourselves to others and have this internal chaos with how we view ourselves but it has nothing to do with other people and everything to do with our own mindset.

I've created a person within myself that I cannot stomach. She's unmotivated, undetermined and uneducated. But is that real?

We're afraid to admit this so we never tackle it. We can't change what we refuse to see.

—Somewhere far, but I hope close.—

I imagine
When you left
You were reborn again
But in new eyes, hair and skin.
And you get to live the new life
You've always said you wanted

...From the beginning again.

Saeed Dozier

I don't need to prove
Anything
To anyone,
Ever.

gave birth to me

but not the reason i exist
gave birth
but not the reason for success
I denounce living vicariously through my breath
When my lungs
Fight for me
And me only

b r e a t h e

*Processes*
Colored solid
Are darkened with past ailments
And sprinkled with current
Pains.
It forces locked doors,
Sweep dirty floors,
And mend every piece
Of you torn.

*Processes*
Colored lightly
Are bright with improvement
And sprinkled with many
Smiles.
It takes everything of you,
A task everyday gone,
And mend every piece
Of you torn.

My feelings aren't here to be liked
They exist to be felt
The outwards liking or disliking
of what's truth to me
Is none of my business

Forgiveness is always for self
Darling,
And you only.
Allow yourself to let go
Of what's holding you down.
The weight that lifts off of you
Feels better than
Anything:
Any pain you felt,
Any disappointment you carried,
Any let downs you experienced.
When you forgive.

I jump the pot
Into fire.

I stop my seed.
Upset that it
Isn't growing at the pace
That I'm comfortable with.

Sometimes I have no say
In my growth.
It's already planned out for me,

and
So

I'll drink my water.

   *the pot meets the plant*

Better the devil you know than the one you don't know?

People have a problem healing because the trauma is familiar

And it's easier to be

comfortable

I can tell you what my best decision was
But then
You'd miss out
On me
Showing you,
On me
Living it,
On me
Being it.

That the life we live
just like the hunger games
is a fight for survival
with pairing savagery

Heavily entertained
As if
Suffering, destruction, pain
is a
Joke

But
You are superior to the anchor
You're not what engulfs you
You are not the struggle that engulfs you
You are not the pain that engulfs you

So
Release.

As I shed
What I used to be
I can only shiver
In gratitude.
I rise
In my new formed
Attitude.

*it's a new day*

Gotta work and let go in order to make space to allow in.

choosing what's best
For mind
in not for out
Liberated,
I am.
It just took some time
To get here.

Thankful for every
Lesson.
Every beckon
That brought me to my lowest
for others,
At the expense of
My peace of mind.

Not anymore.

I am the change.

They said be patient
because
everything will come
And the universe will give it

to you

with just one thought

b r e a t h e

POETREE

# VIII

# Eyes wide Open

Learning from my own mistakes
Gave me a gate
With a lock
and a key,
That I had all along,
I just refused to use it.

I bet
We are just stories
Made up
From other beings
Outside of the globe.
We entertain,
We draw pain,
replicate,
& Rotate in disdain.

*beyond what we are taught*

I am happy because of me.

I can't wait on others
Or I'll be waiting
for the rest of my life.

I love to hear your laugh
and see your genuine smiles
but Sometimes you leave
With a part in your mind
hidden behind a door.
not in terror
Or Weeping
But You stand.
become it,
Built Strong
With many weapons.
Prepared for anything that can bust
Through
Uninvited.

But
Sometimes
I'm Afraid to approach
For fear of a disaster.

You leave
And I cannot recognize you.

Just a stranger in your face.

I want those laughs and smiles back.

*self*

the point is not to be attached

I am not any other definition
Outside of what I say
And that may change
When I say
I am not an aesthetic
A vibe or a look
I am not what's outside of me
I am inside
I am the unseeable
The untouchable
the incomprehensible

it's required to
Close your eyes
to see me
&
Hold yourself
To feel me

Do we have time for our inner voice? Higher self?

I trust you to be exactly who you are

    vs

    I trust you to not hurt me

        **only one is truth**

There is no separation
everything exists
mashed
smashed
Into each other
messy

And heavy

Love doesn't work
When you force it,
When you look for it.
It works when you are being it
When it finds *you*.

Not filled with glamour or glitter
Far from privilege
Or luxury
But lots of pain,
Confusion
Suffering
And struggle
filled

Not all
But too much
I am still healing from this
And so
I'm taking my time

You
show
And
then
I
de-
ter-
mine
whet
her I
can take
on
what
you put
out
And
then
I
move
on or
not.

As parallel to earth
            we are to our shadow self

Goodbyes

are said
To the people,
Never to the memories.
or the feelings trapped within them

when everything you do
is only rooted in physical
beauty
    a countdown is put on
your existence
    because beauty is subjective
    and aging is inevitable

    What        is
under    neath?

yes,
my love has conditions
And they are
dressed as boundaries

I forgave you
For being a part of the hurt that happened.
then forgave myself
for not letting it go

and so


Grief,

a price too heavy to pay
the effervescence of pain .

The only way out
Is so deeply through.
Face your ailments,
Your fears,
And pains
Then
Let it all go.

Yet, I live today confidently
because every part
of *my* ecosystem
has a vital role in making the whole that is me.

happiness over anything.
If you cared too
There'd be no need to choose.

Lately,
　I've just been breathing in the moment
　holding on to chosen time
　Cause I'll never know when the last will leave.
　I just listen to the leaves
　Rustle
　make sure i don't fumble
　Or tumble
　On too many steps forward
　because I'll be falling forever.
　If I don't get that smile up
　These eyes won't have the style
　Of wisdom
　And that's all I need

　Wisdom

being aware is what i want
                For right or wrong
neither matters.

awareness
To recognize
realize
And rectify;
repair.

That's the path.

with no awareness comes no accountability

Love is respect.
Protect yourself at all costs.

Respect yourself at all costs.

no character develop-
ment?

  no emotional reg-
ulation

    no awareness

    no connection

a playground for turmoil.

Is this something I can grow with or just tolerate?
Is toleration growth?
Is it a reflection of character?
Or a reflection of awareness?
Or lack thereof?
Is it compatible?
palpable?
Most of all does it
add to my happiness?

**The moment I feel**
I have to prove myself

I will remove myself

Walking between raindrops
Divine are your steps.
Balance between all energies
Exuding limitless power.
Power to lift Kings & Queens,
Royalty,
Divine,
I say.

...just captivated

wrapped in the juiciness
Soft
Tenderness
Of brown sugar.

Feeling
Like the hairs all over
stand up tall.
Feeling
Like a warm back rub,

Splashed
On the beach or
A sip of
piping
Hot
camomile tea.

Overwhelming.
This body
You see.
Is godly....

I'm still learning myself because
it's an ever growing journey

with no real end

*forever a student*

I don't think it's about the amount, more or less, of love anymore. Everyone holds all love languages, some weighing more than others. Can't be loved as you were in the past or even be loved the same in the present because as time moves so do others... Your wants and needs may not be the same all the time and it's okay to love and receive love differently. Love is still love. There is no one definition.

I go with what respects me
And if i even have to ask
I don't want it

I deserve to be respected
To be safe
To be heard
To be seen
To be considered
I want to be remembered

figured and configured
like the puzzle I am
gently handled
like the puzzle I am

**I just am**
What i am
When i am
How i am

Thinking
and thoughtless
At the same time

advice on healing?

1) keep asking questions. give yourself the opportunity to discover more. 2) Take your time. wounds can be so deep that it affects our spiritual code and dna. I still have trauma lingering in me that affected my grandmother. 3) Let yourself feel everything and feel the ugly ones too. going through a healing of this sort will bring guilt, shame, anger, resentment, revengeful or even hateful feelings. feel it, then 4) Let it go. Take time to be silent with yourself so that you rebuild your spiritual cells. 5) some say give forgiveness but take your time.

Our Eyes are for seeing
I hope you use them
Differentiate dreams from reality
I hope you use them

How difficult it is
                to face myself
In the waking hours of
                Self-awareness.
How hard it is
                To face my flaws.
How hard it is
                To let go.
How hard it is
                To get better.

Finally the mercy of *epiphany*

You never received all you deserved as a child

from yours

or them from theirs.


So I'm entangled
in a trickled effect of an already
Broken record.
I'm what's left     of the storms
That passed

If I can grab it
Hold it
Grow it
I can give it to my future children

**Never let anything keep you from your dreams**

Lost in a reality
I'm trembling in a fractional and transactional world.
The actual
Facts of life
Lie dormant in what we think is fantasy.
So I'm stuck in universal limbo
With limbs that nimble
Two fourths (2/4) faithful after every revolution.
Because INdividual cracks the leading.
If you read these words, or any words,
and draw no conclusions,
Are you really reading?

**Learned**

People love outwardly
To the capacity of their own self love

People only communicate
to the degree of their own self-awareness

**and**

Behavior only
reflects the level of unhealed or healed trauma

When my creativity is directly connected
And reflecting
Truth
        Then i can truly be

Myself
    Free
        Satisfied
            Fulfilled

Anything less
Leave
A big gaping hole

In my heart of hearts

**I live in this existence but**
                              **I do not subscribe to it**

Everything has an equation
To solve
Except
           Awareness.

in the present
There is no equation
But just
to be.

But everything around us
are perfect distractions
And Pull us
Further
And further away
From the present

Spoiled food in the fridge = wrong people around you
Why'd it spoil? = lack of attention, awareness, care
How to prevent it = recognition + change

Fresh food in the fridge = healthier people around you
What's the difference? = awareness

*Intention + action*

blocked by Fear? (surrender)
 blocked by Guilt? (forgive)
  blocked by Shame? (must not deny parts of self. self-acceptance)
   blocked by Grief? (release. love is in all forms)
    blocked by Lies? (trust yourself. be authentic)
     blocked by Illusion? (everything is connected)
      blocked by Earthly Attachment? ( detachment is balance)

Don't force the delusion
in order to pacify the pain that comes with this truth

*a poet*
with more layers
too many to explain
is better to feel in person
to see what they see 1st person
to show what they're made of
and show others they're made of same cloth

*this poet*
bottom isn't the right description for
where she's from
but showing who she is
pairing her voice with any picture
showing what she can do
is enough for the people

*that poet*
wishes the world could see the world how they see it
treat it how they treat it
But is fine with teaching
and so
exploration for them
is mind, body and soul

a poet, this poet, that poet
promise to deliver it in gold

My entire perspective on fear changed when
I decided to conquer one

*Fear lasts for 3 seconds*

I was told
When you have a claim
You should also have a proof
reference
Because
Without one
It's just opinion
And opinion is a feeling
And feelings aren't always
Fact

Negative
thoughts
are like
the first cells of a
disease

**The weight of radical self love and self care**
Always look like betrayal
To others
Who know not how that looks

Everything is a reflection of you

> We are a *part* of evolution. We are not the evolution

**The end point is the "reward" for the journey.**
It's to show and recognize what was done in order to reach that end. The point is not the prize. It's a reminder of what you went through because the reward lasts for 5 seconds.

I don't want to rush through my journey for 5 seconds of relief.
I want to encapsulate myself into each step
so that when I get to that end,
    the top, the goal.
I can take a deep breath of gratitude and then move on.

**Poe in NYC 2020**
*photographed by tonibakalli*

Poetree, Poe for short, is a multidisciplinary artist from Newark, New Jersey, born to a Black and Indigenous (Chippewa & Blackfoot) mother and a Puerto Rican father. Poe is proudly a first generation graduate with a BA in English Language & Literature and Sociology with a concentration in Social Deviance from Saint Peter's University. Throughout her youth she experienced many traumas and struggles from sexual, mental and physical abuse, homelessness, familial and neighborhood violence and death, to witnessing drug abuse and the effects it had on her own community and family. These experiences paired with her desire to break generational cycles encouraged her to lean on art to cope and heal from the aspects of her life she could not control.

From formal dance training starting at 9 years old, writing her very first poem at just 11 years old, to obtaining multiple Literary Magazine publications by the time she reached adulthood, Poe evolved over the years as an artreprenur, dancer, poet, model and artist. The force of exhibiting her take on beauty expression, culture, naturalism, activism, feminism and the power of her art, "being unapologetically herself," through social media led to features in Essence, Elle, Refinery29, Byrdie, BET, Revolt TV and much more.

Poe is currently based in Los Angeles, California, working on producing and directing her debut poetry album with an accompanying film.

You can keep up with her at *www.poetreethefeminist.com*.

www.ingramcontent.com/pod-product-compliance
Lightning Source LLC
Chambersburg PA
CBHW050331010526
**44119CB00004B/123**